# THE SIMPLE HOME

JULIA BIRD · PHOTOGRAPHS BY PIA TRYDE

# THE SIMPLE HOME

## DECORATING WITH WHITE, CREAM & NATURAL MATERIALS

EBURY PRESS
LONDON

FOR GUM

First published 1995

1 3 5 7 9 10 8 6 4 2

Text copyright © Ebury Press 1995

Photography copyright © Pia Tryde 1995

First published in the United Kingdom in 1995 by Ebury Press

Random House, 20 Vauxhall Bridge Road, London SW1V 2SA

Random House Australia (Pty) Limited

20 Alfred Street, Milsons Point, Sydney,

New South Wales 2061, Australia

Random House New Zealand Limited

18 Poland Road, Glenfield, Auckland 10, New Zealand

Random House South Africa (Pty) Limited

PO Box 337, Bergvlei, South Africa

Random House UK Limited Reg. No. 954009

A CIP catalogue record for this book is available from the British Library.

Text by EMMA CALLERY

Designed by GEORGINA RHODES

Styling Assistance: LIVIA FRANCIS, OLIVIA CLARK

Illustrations: PETER HORRIDGE (openers),

DAVID DOWNTON (step-by-steps),

STEPHEN DEW (templates)

Typesetting by RICHARD PROCTOR

ISBN 009 180811 1

Colour reproduction by Colorlito Rigogliosi s.r.l., Milan

Printed and bound in Italy by New Interlitho Italia S.p.a., Milan

# CONTENTS

## AFTER-DINNER MINTS

*Here a bowl of refreshing*

*after-dinner mints are pictured*

*with a treasured French*

*bonbon box.*

# INTRODUCTION

The simple home is about living with ease, space and light – an altogether therapeutic way to live. It is honest in its pared down, pure state, and is simply created by using whites and natural materials as the foundations for each room. Within this framework other colours can then be introduced according to the season and how your mood fluctuates. There are times when I find great comfort in the calm of old, muted whites, creams and woody tones highlighted by a vividly pink peony picked fresh from the garden. Or I may feel the need to inject more colour into a room to warm it up for winter – with a pair of bright lime green linen curtains, say – or freshen it for the first days of summer with an indigo blue quilt. The wonderful thing about decorating within a neutral framework is that you will never feel constrained by the complexities of colour coordination.

Keeping up with the current ultimate in interior accessories has become an exhausting and expensive process. This is when you start valuing what is simple and naturally available around you. I find that I now achieve far more satisfaction in elevating household basics such as a ball of string from the kitchen drawer and working it into a decorative braid to trim a curtain, or bringing an old galvanized bucket indoors and filling it with an armful of seasonal flowering lilac. Likewise, rejuvenating inexpensive oddities from local junk shops into something entirely useful or purely decorative, is very rewarding. Ultimately, it is all about developing a style that you feel comfortable with. I hope this book will inspire you to transform your home both simply and naturally.

JULIA BIRD

## SIMPLICITY

*The simple purity of a single*

*flower standing in a glass vase*

*is all that a dinner table needs*

*to complete the setting.*

the same, matching fabric for all of your cushions; by varying the texture and style, white is brought to life. The simplest of cushions can be made from plain cotton finished with lengths of piping around the edges, or for a more crumpled look wash linen and then leave it to dry naturally before making it up into cushions of different shapes and sizes. For window seats, make deep, comfortable squab cushions from worn-out old quilts – remember to use any holey bits on the underside. For added effect, seek out old pieces of Indian fabric thickly embroidered with cotton and tiny mirrors, and make up the prettiest pieces into cushions.

Chair covers can be made as simple or complicated as you like, but closely fitted covers are usually the preserve of the upholsterer. Loose fitting covers, however, are more readily achievable as long as you make a plan on dressmaker's layout paper for the dimensions of each piece first. Then pin, fit and cut the sections in place on the chair before finally sewing the cover together. For that added decorative detail, add piping all around the edges. After all this work you won't want to have to make another cover in a hurry, so always use a robust fabric that will last for many years. The most suitable fabrics are medium-heavyweight cottons, linens and damask weaves.

A more straightforward loose chair cover can be made by covering the seat only. Cut sufficient fabric to cover the seat and the depth of each edge, adding seam allowances too. Neaten the edges, shape the fabric at the front corners with stitched seams and add a length of cotton tape to each corner for tying. Then simply slip the cover over the seat and tie in place under each leg with the tapes. There are some incredibly beautiful quilted white on white fabrics available but their prices can be prohibitive – so this sort of cover is the ideal way to feature a piece in your home as it requires only a metre (yard) or less.

With the simplest made blinds it is the finishing touches that add to their

PREVIOUS PAGE

SOFT TONES

*A sun-bleached, bright white*

*beach house has been*

*tempered by hues of soft*

*grey, cream, pink and buff,*

*ensuring an easy and*

*comfortable look.*

LEFT

WINTER WARMTH

*A warm, off-white painted wall*

*combined with rustic rush*

*flooring creates a cosy winter*

*ambience.*

PREVIOUS PAGE

## PANELLED CUSHIONS

*Unusual cushions of crisp*

*linen have been cleverly*

*engineered into pleated*

*panels.*

LEFT

## HIDING THE DEFECTS

*A damaged chair seat can*

*be concealed with a simple*

*cotton cover, secured*

*with ties made from the*

*same fabric.*

interest. Ring pulls made from wooden curtain rings tied on with tape, or a small collection of beach twigs tied together with raffia, are so easy to make, and yet so stylish. On the blinds themselves, consider adding a pretty scalloped effect to the edge of a printed voile blind; or make Roman blinds from the plainest, simplest cotton. When pulled up, these blinds fall in loose gathers that have the most attractive shadows when the sun pours through. Alternatively, to achieve some of that Mediterranean simplicity, use very fine slatted blinds or hang delicate lace panels, soft muslin or cheesecloth over the windows.

### NATURAL FLOORING

If you have floorboards in your living room, these are the perfect setting for a simply decorated interior. To enhance the wood grain of floorboards and at the same time give them a soft-white tint, apply a liming paste. First stroke the wood with a wire brush, gently working in the direction of the grain. Then apply the liming paste with some fine steel wool, making sure you fill in the grain as you work. Rub in a circular motion over small areas at a time, and allow the

ABOVE

## MARBLED BOXES

*Recycle old and tatty filing*

*boxes by covering them with*

*marbled art paper, stuck in*

*place with paper adhesive.*

*The ties are made from*

*lengths of cotton tape that*

*are fed into deep slits made*

*with a scalpel in the box tops*

*and bottoms. They are then*

*secured with a strip of*

*adhesive tape.*

LEFT

## MIXED CONTAINERS

*A hallway arrangement will*

*present an immediate impact*

*as you walk through the front*

*door. Keep it simple – here*

*galvanized buckets used as*

*containers to hold a small*

*bunch of flowers contrast*

*beautifully with the speckled*

*glass 'flower-pot' vases.*

# LEAFY LAMPSHADE

**WHAT YOU WILL NEED**

200gsm white card

Lamp fitting

Carbon paper

Soft pencil

Craft knife

Cutting mat

Sewing machine

White cotton thread

Double-sided tape

Needle

Scissors

12mm (½in)-wide gummed

linen tape

1 Use fairly stiff white card for the background and decoration on this lampshade and either re-use an existing lamp fitting or buy an appropriately sized one – an upper ring fitted with a mounting ring will be sufficient. To make the shade, enlarge the template on pages 184-5 to an appropriate size on a photocopier, transfer to the back of the card using carbon paper and soft pencil, and then cut out the card using the craft knife on the cutting mat. Ensure that you allow 12mm (½in) overlap at the ends so that the shade can be stuck together easily. It is important that you make the top and bottom edges as smooth as possible so that the finished effect is neat. Prepare and cut out as many leaves as you require in the same way.

2 Thread up a sewing machine with ordinary white cotton thread and then stitch the stems onto the background using the largest stitch. To avoid as much finishing off as possible, stitch backwards and forwards three times, making the stems flowing as freely as you like. If you are worried about stitching without guidelines, lightly draw some on the card before starting using a very soft pencil. These can easily be rubbed off once you have finished. Don't finish off your thread, but keep stitching straight into step 3.

3 For the leaf detailing, start sewing at the end of the stem that you have reached and every now and then position a card leaf on the background and stitch over this to attach it. To keep the leaves in place while stitching, use a tiny piece of double-sided tape or hold in place with your fingers. Continue the line of stitching from leaf to leaf and finish off by cutting the

## THE LAMPSHADE

*Simple leaf shapes are cut*

*out and stitched into place*

*freestyle.*

cotton leaving about 15cm (6in) excess. Then stitch the top thread through to the back using a sewing needle.

4 To make the lampshade, join the ends together using double-sided tape. Overlap the edges sufficiently so that the ring of the fitting falls just below the top edge of the lampshade. Use the gummed linen tape to finish the top and bottom edges. Although expensive, this tape is perfect for the job as it stretches, so making a smooth finish around the curved edges easier to obtain. Measure two lengths of tape around the edges of the lampshade and add 2.5cm (1in) allowance. Then dampen down and leave for a few minutes to soften so that it becomes pliable. Fold one length neatly over the bottom edge with 6mm ($\frac{1}{4}$in) on each side. Stick it along the outside edge first and then carefully and slowly fold the excess over to the inside. Repeat along the top, but this time ensure that you catch the lampshade ring within the tape on the inside.

## STORAGE BOXES

*Crisp white bonbon boxes are*

*perfect for gifts or*

*chocolates, or for storing bits*

*and pieces such as a*

*collection of button, stamps*

*or beads.*

# BONBON BOXES

**WHAT YOU WILL NEED**

Fairly stiff white card

Stiffened white card

Scissors

Scalpel

Metal ruler

Large needle

PVA glue or double-sided

tape

1.2m (4ft) raffia, string

or cord

4 x 2.5cm (1in)-diameter

sticky circles (optional)

1 Using the templates on pages 182-3 cut out each box and base piece from the white card. The card should not be too stiff because it needs to be fairly flexible, but neither should it be too flimsy as the box needs to hold its shape. Should you want to make larger or smaller boxes, enlarge or reduce the template on a photocopier as appropriate. Also cut out a piece of stiffened card to fit in the bottom. Lightly score along the tab fold lines with a scalpel and metal ruler.

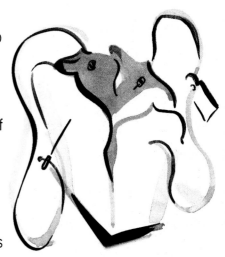

*Making the raffia loops*

2 The box will ultimately be tied together with coloured raffia through holes in the sides of the box. Punch out the holes where marked on the template using the needle. Then carefully glue or stick the tabs onto all four sides of the base piece of card and glue the stiffened card onto the bottom to disguise the tabs.

3 Cut two 60cm (24in) lengths of the coloured raffia and to make the loops, thread each end into the box through the holes using the needle and knot at the inside. For a more utilitarian finish, use string, or for a really chic effect, use gold cord. If you want to add a label to the box, thread it onto one of the loops before making the second knot. To neatly finish off the inside, cover each knot with one of the round sticky labels.

*Closing the bonbon box*

4 To close the box, fold down the small side flaps first, then the long flaps, one on top of the other. Draw up the raffia loops to the middle of the top of the box and twist to give some control before tying in a pretty bow.

# CHAPTER TWO

# ROOMS FOR DINING

# ROOMS FOR DINING

Eating is one of the greatest of past-times. Sitting at an informally laid table with a group of friends, eating simple fare and drinking good wine, has to be one of the most relaxing of activities. And how better to enhance this treat, than by sitting in a restrainedly decorated room surrounded by charmingly grouped treasures and stored china and linen?

Shelves and cupboards are the obvious places in which to keep your china and glass in dining rooms, and at the same time they can be utilized to display your collections. Take pride in your belongings, show them off. If at all possible, erect simple shelving or search out a glass-fronted display cabinet and then set about filling the shelves with a collection of china and glassware. Whites mix together beautifully, so do not worry about having non-matching sets; add a jug here, a tureen there, and incorporate a range of patterns. The French make simple china so successfully. The plates tend to be generously large and the bowls can be cupped in the hand, and as such are frequently used for drinking breakfast coffee. Also, by no means are all pieces of china round; there are angular coffee cups, and octagonal plates – such a refreshing change. China with embossed patterns sit very comfortably alongside plates with fluted edges, and with this freedom it will take you next to no time to collect ceramics from all manner of places.

Obviously, if you are mounting your own shelving you need to make sure that it is very firmly fixed so that your valuable collections do not come crashing down to the ground. Once they are in place, decide whether you want to paint them to match the rest of the woodwork in the room, or perhaps go for a subtle stain or limewash (see page 87). Whichever finish you decide on, prepare the

LEFT

## MIXED MATERIALS

*This unusual and stylish sideboard has been made by placing a marble top on to an old, rusty wrought-iron base. Alternatively, a glass table top would look extremely effective. A Victorian glass display case holds a stack of seed and bean balls, while a pile of glass plates and painted glasses await a table-setting. The whole effect is dramatically expanded by standing the table beside a floor-to-ceiling mirror.*

## SIMPLE DISPLAYS

Here a glass-fronted display cupboard has been decorated with a distressed paint effect and then filled in a charmingly casual way. Piles of linen tablecloths and napkins feature beneath a mis-matching set of fluted white china. The back of the cupboard has been used to good effect by leaning several of the larger plates against it.

## ALL STRUNG UP

To prevent the piles of linen napkins from becoming an unruly heap of fabric, lengths of good plain string have been neatly tied around each set, parcel-like. Alternatively, use pieces of raffia, or lengths of cotton tape.

## A PRESSED GLASS COLLECTION

*This beautifully carved shelf*

*unit has been painted with a*

*matt finish which works well*

*with this collection of*

*decorated pressed glass lids.*

*Emulating cut glass, these*

*lids are relatively cheap to*

*buy and, of course, can be*

*put to good practical use*

*protecting food in the larder*

*or for outdoor entertaining.*

*To add a dash of colour, a*

*couple of brightly coloured*

*postcards have been propped*

*up on the bottom shelf.*

RIGHT

## TIME FOR TEA

*Crisp white china and a good old-fashioned glass cake stand is the perfect vehicle for displaying wrapped buns for tea.*

RIGHT

## COFFEE BREAK

*The hard lines of the classic chequered black and white floor tiles sharply contrast with the soft white painted walls and cupboard.*

surface first by lightly sanding it and then remove the dust by wiping over the shelves with a cloth dampened in white spirit.

Side tables and deep windowsills are equally wonderful places on which to group other collections that you feel sit happily in a dining room, or for a strong impact carefully position one particularly cherished item. For something a little more unusual, make seed and bean balls like those featured on pages 53 and 70-3, and group them together on a beautiful platter.

## DRESSING TABLES

A well-dressed table is a sight to behold, and it needn't be anything too complicated or time-consuming to create. With the aid of a length of natural linen sheeting you can make a crisp tablecloth with matching napkins; then lay on top piles of china, cutlery and glasses awaiting a table-setting. A simple floral arrangement or two will complete the picture.

Tablecloths can be as plain or as ornate as you like. Every now and then treat yourself to a particularly beautiful cloth to lay across your table – it will

RIGHT

## LET THE OUTSIDE IN

When the sun shines, throw
the doors open wide and
bring your dining table
forward to greet the day. The
garden chairs further
emphasize the sense of the
great outdoors, while the
chandelier hanging above the
table and the crisp linen
tablecloth add a lovely sense
of occasion. The muslin
curtains have been neatly tied
back with cotton tape to
make the most of the view
and gently diffuse the strong
sunlight.

certainly make you and any fellow diners feel special. For a simple decorative touch, use a linen cloth stitched with drawn threadwork and embroidery. Or create a fine piece of frippery by laying a linen sheet over the table, catching it up at each corner and securing in place with a couple of ties stitched so that they can be knotted together. The end result is a very flirty tablecloth – and so simple to make too.

For more informal occasions, bring in dining chairs from all around the house, even those wire garden chairs garnered from the junk shop around the corner. A matching set of dining chairs is not necessarily a prerequisite of a good meal, and a miscellaneous collection will certainly add a sense of the unusual to the setting.

## LAYING THE TABLE

Pile soup bowls on top of fish plates on top of dinner plates and for absolute simplicity just have one set of knife and fork for each person laid with the fork prongs facing down onto the cloth. Cut glass alongside engraved vessels looks great – as with the china, don't worry overly much about matching sets. A table laid with variety suggests a carefree spirit.

Next to each setting, position a linen napkin neatly folded in a rectangle, nothing more ornate is needed. Make your own by cutting up some fabric remnants and either neatly hem around the edges, or make a small fringe by stitching 2.5cm (1in) in from the edge and gently pulling out the loose threads. For a slightly unusual touch, use monogrammed hand towels found in antique shops, or stitch your own letters in cross stitch copying a style of lettering to suit your own taste – there are many embroidery books that feature such alphabets, and transfers are available from needlework shops.

Dining by candlelight has to be the most romantic setting. White candles

FOLLOWING PAGE

ENGRAVED
GLASSES

*A group of decoratively engraved glasses is simple to put together and the end result is so delicate and attractive. A small glass makes the perfect holder for a single fragrant rose.*

## TABLE DRESSING

*The prettiest side table is covered with a coarse un-bleached linen cloth which has been caught up at each corner and secured with tape tied in a bow. An exquisite panel of embroidered muslin helps diffuse the late afternoon sun and disguise an ugly view.*

## WHITE ON WHITE

*White on white ceramics on cream linen: a true evocation of the success of decorating with pale colours. The textures of these contrasting materials work so well together and they are a testament to simple dining.*

# BEAN BALLS

**WHAT YOU WILL NEED**

Florist's foam balls

Dried *haricots blancs,*

or similar

Hot glue gun

Narrow cotton braid, cord

or string (40cm [18in]

per ball)

1 Use balls of florist's foam as the basis for this creamy, textured variation on the traditional pomander. These balls can be bought in various sizes, but whether you choose to use a mixture of sizes or make several all of the same size depends on what final effect you are intending to achieve. Here, the bean balls are two different sizes.

2 The balls are then covered with the dried *haricots blancs* stuck in place with the hot glue gun. Stick on the beans one by one, putting the hot glue on the end of each. Firmly press in place on the foam and gradually work your way all around the ball.

3 You needn't feel limited to using the *haricots blancs* alone. There are so many different coloured dried beans available that you might choose to work in different colours across the ball creating patterns such as stripes, spirals or spots of varying colour, or for a more subtle effect, just add the occasional darker coloured bean to the *haricots blancs*. To enhance the textural quality of these balls, use dried beans in assorted sizes and shapes as well as colours.

4 To finish off, tie a length of narrow cotton braid, cord or string twice around each ball at ninety-degrees to each other – like a pomander – and finish off neatly at the top with a bow. Again, for some variation, leave the occasional ball ribbon-free so that their deliciously tactile textures can be appreciated in their entirety.

# FLORAL FLOORCLOTH

**WHAT YOU WILL NEED**

Heavy duty artist's canvas

Dressmaker's scissors

Large needle

White buttonhole thread

PVA glue

Acrylic paints (white,

ochre)

Soft pencil

Paintbrushes

(2.5cm (1in) wide, artist's)

Masking tape

Acrylic varnish (glossy

or matt)

1 Cut the canvas to size using the dressmaker's scissors. Allow an extra 10cm (4in) around each edge for the hem. To make the hem, fold the edges over to the back twice, each time folding 5cm (2in), and press.

2 At each corner make a neat mitre. To do this, unfold the turnings and cut across the corner diagonally where the first turn creases meet. Align the folded corner along the second turning creases and press. Then refold the hems along the fold lines with the corner folded inside the hems, stitch down the corners and then glue the hems with the PVA glue.

3 Paint the canvas all over with white acrylic paint – acrylic paints don't crack easily, so don't worry about painting too thick a layer. Then mark out the design (in this case, a floral border) with a soft pencil. Either copy the design given on pages 178-9, or draw your own.

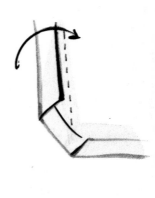

RIGHT

*Preparing the border*

FAR RIGHT

*Mitring the corners*

4 Paint the design mixing the acrylic paints to achieve different shades of ochre and use the 2.5cm (1in) paintbrush for filling in the background and artist's brushes for the details. Leave the paint to dry. The dark lines within the border are painted freehand over pencil drawn guidelines. For the dark ochre surround, stick masking tape 3.5cm (1½in) in from the edge of the floorcloth and paint all the way around. Leave to dry and carefully remove the tape to reveal a neat, crisp finish. Finally, paint at least three coats of glossy or matt acrylic varnish over the top side to seal it.

limestone tiles, each of which have their own distinctive character and colouring, bringing with them the cool, continental style that is simple and stylish.

For a spot of Provençal decor, search out plain hexagonal, square or rectangular tiles. You can find them in all shapes, sizes and colours ranging from rich reds to soft pinks and orange tones. When mixed at random on a floor, they will give a tremendous warmth, perfectly complementing the coolness of white walls and woodwork.

## WHITENING WALLS AND WOODWORK

Tongue-and-groove boarding on the walls is a familiar feature in many cultures. From New England to Scandinavia, the hard-wearing and insulating properties of such interlocking cladding have been appreciated for centuries. It is relatively simple to erect on straight walls, more complicated on surfaces that are uneven. The success of such boarding relies on the accurate fixing of horizontal battens at regular intervals up the wall. The tongue-and-groove panels are then slotted one into another and nailed to the battens to secure them to the wall. An unrelieved expanse of wood on the walls, however, can be overpowering and so once in place, prepare and paint the boarding in the usual way – a wash of paint is the most popular treatment.

Whites and creams painted onto walls give an impression of brightness and spaciousness. A coat of paint on a ceiling will make it look higher, and a pristine, white wall in a kitchen is perfect for displaying things on, whether they be collections of paintings or chrome kitchen utensils. But don't feel restricted to using white on all the surfaces in the kitchen – a dash of Gustavian blue stencilling, or some lemon yellow woodwork not only looks effective but also relieves the potential intensity of white everywhere. There are various ways of achieving the creamy mellow, lived-in tones of old distemper, limewash and

LEFT

IN THE LARDER
*Beautiful hand-woven rush baskets from the south of France make great storage containers for vegetables in the coolness of a whitewashed larder.*

LEFT

## WOODEN PANELLING

*Tongue-and-groove boarding painted with reflective glossy paint enhances this small kitchen. Simple shelves have been added above the cupboards and are used to house a mixture of enamel and tin storage jars and various aged and shapely tin kitchen paraphernalia.*

FOLLOWING PAGE

## COOL AND CLEAN

*The old-fashioned larder cupboard featuring zinc mesh panels is both practical and good looking for general kitchen storage.*

LEFT

## STORAGE SPACE

*A pretty white panelled cupboard holds a store of preserves. The shelves are trimmed with lengths of lace-effect paper ribbon.*

whitewash – the materials traditionally used on walls. The simplest solution is to mix a touch of raw sienna artist's oil paint or powder into white eggshell paint. This takes off the glare and gives it a creamy, slightly yellow hue.

Alternatively, limewash gives a soft, translucent finish and it is very easy to mix and apply. Lime stirred into a plastic bucket three-quarters filled with water is all that is required. The consistency should be of thick cream and then after leaving it to stand for three days it can be strained and diluted once again. To colour the limewash, add water-based colour such as artist's acrylic paints, poster paints, or cement dyes. Add a little at a time until you achieve the colour you require, but remember that the mixed colour is much lighter once dry.

For a softly patterned, subtle and translucent finish apply a water-based

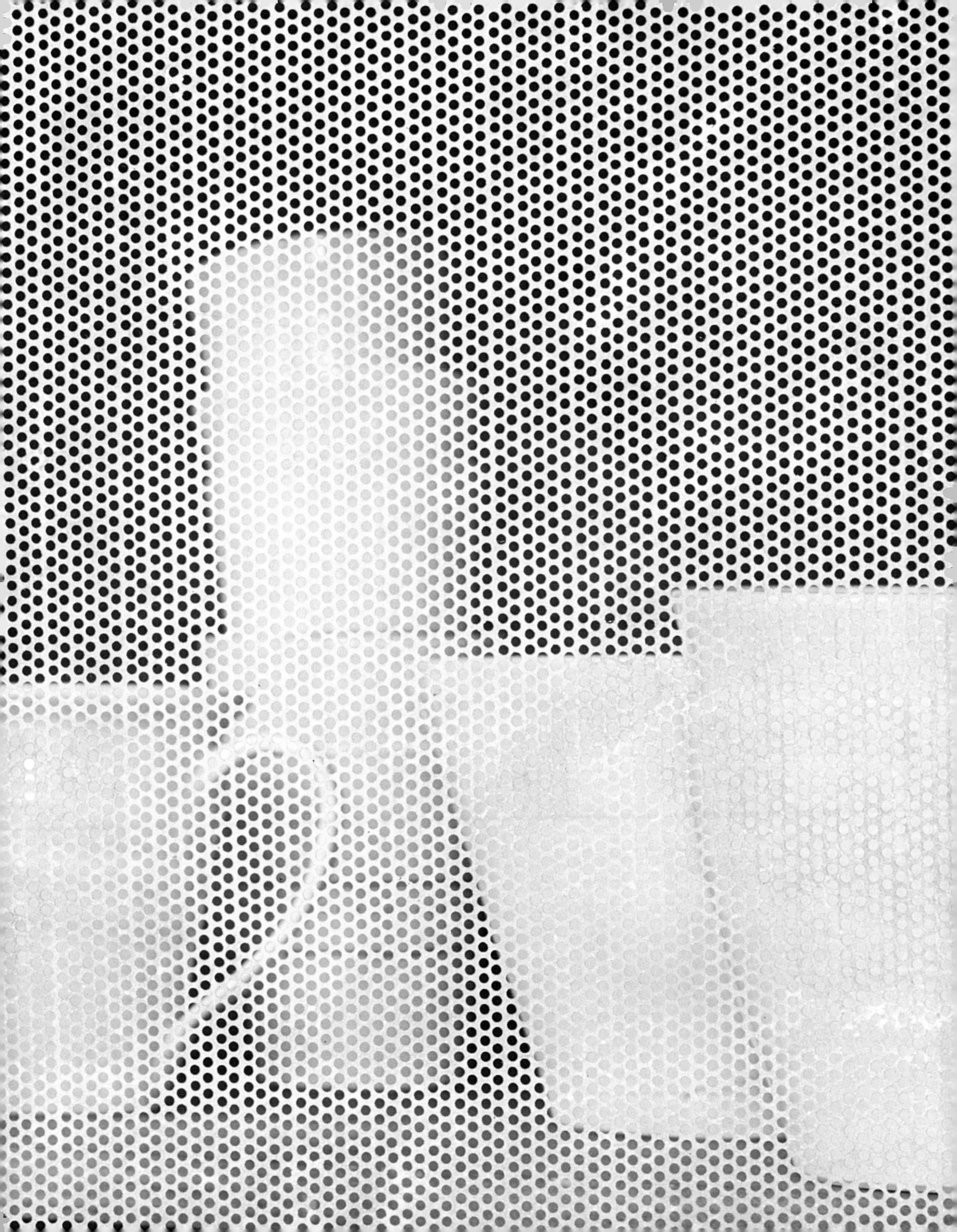

LEFT

## LIGHTENING A KITCHEN

*The palest grey paintwork sets off the hard stone stainless steel cooker achieving a calm and elegant basement kitchen. Open shelving houses essential day-to-day needs stored in smart chrome-lidded jars.*

LEFT

## ALL WASHED UP

*Refreshingly modern chrome cutlery with its clear plastic handles works beautifully with this pierced edged china, retaining a sense of clarity.*

wash over a white emulsion background. To make an emulsion wash, dilute one part of emulsion with four parts of water, adding some powder colour for a subtle tinge (see page 105). Apply the wash with broad sweeps of the paintbrush to small areas at a time. Then soften it with a damp brush by lightly passing it over the emulsion a few times during the drying process. Distemper was the standard paint in Europe and the USA until the 1950s, but a colourwash such as this is just as effective and the covering qualities are far better.

## AGEING EFFECTS

If you are blessed with perfectly smooth walls and want to create something a little more crumbly and decayed, it is perfectly possible to make your own ageing plaster wall. First coat the wall with PVA mixed with water in equal quantities and then leave it to dry. Next heat equal quantities of beeswax polish and turpentine in a bain-marie and, when cooled, brush on the wall in patches at random. While the wax is still soft, apply a thin layer of white gypsum plaster with a trowel in broad sweeps until the wall is completely covered. As it sets, splash water onto the plaster with a brush and then remove ridges and obvious marks with a wetted trowel. To loosen the plaster over the waxed areas, leave the plaster to dry for a day and then knock with a hammer (wear eye protection) and scrape away any excess plaster. Finally, sand the surface lightly and paint on a coat of diluted PVA to protect it.

Likewise, on wooden furniture or any other wooden surface, a waxed finish successfully replicates the look of aged milk paint. The buffed wax gives a sheen to the paint and also acts as a sealant, preventing the flat finish from picking up dirt. Prepare the wood by washing it thoroughly and then gently scrub the surface with a wire brush and rinse again with clean hot water. Leave the wood overnight to dry completely, fill any cracks or holes with wood filler and

LEFT

## THE OLD AND
## THE NEW

*Combining old and new items in a simple setting works really well. In this kitchen, the modern island worksurface made of palest ash sits alongside the galvanized ribbed dustbin, a large cast-iron radiator, and an old zinc-panelled, painted storage cupboard.*

# CHAPTER FOUR

# ROOMS FOR SLEEPING

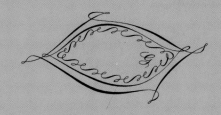

# ROOMS FOR SLEEPING

Of all the rooms in the home, the bedroom is the place where white decoration and fabric can have the most magical effects. Crisp calico and filmy muslin, fine cotton and delicate linen; these are all the stuff of which gentle dreams are made. But don't feel that you have to limit yourself to pure white in any room of your home, particularly the bedroom, where muted shades can be very relaxing. Mix soft pigments into white eggshell or titanium white (an opaque white oil paint), to add a hint of subtlety to the backdrop of your decor. For warm tones add some burnt sienna for a slightly pink tint or raw sienna for a hint of yellow. For a cool, greying white use raw umber. As their names imply, these earth colours originate from Italy and as such the colours they create are redolent of the freshness of southern Europe. Creating exactly the right shade for your room is purely a matter of experimenting and you should always test the colours on a piece of board or lining paper in its location before setting to with a paintbrush on the walls.

But remember, too, that the most important ingredient in a room is the light itself. In each room, the amount constantly varies – at noon, a wooden floor can make a white wall appear softly yellow; but by twilight, the white will be much greyer. So subtly tint your white paints according to what finished effect you intend to achieve in your bedroom.

To further enhance the softness of a bedroom, cover your bed with a simply patterned white quilt and then pile it high with pillows made from linen and old lace. For the bedlinen itself, there is nothing better than climbing into crisp white cotton piqué sheets – there are some truly beautiful sheets to be found, and those embroidered with drawn threadwork add a great sense of chic.

LEFT

LIME GREEN LINEN

*These casual, layered linen curtains in bright chartreuse green inject a flash of colour which, combined with sharpest white, has a truly enlivening effect on the facing bedroom. A junk shop table stands proud with a new lick of paint and it sits happily with the well-worn paintwork of the chair.*

OPPOSITE

## CROWNING GLORY

*Simple drapes of cotton seersucker are hung from a wooden corona – the fabric is simply stapled into place. Fresh linens, lace-edged pillows and a floral-sprigged quilt soften the heaviness of the French Empire bed.*

RIGHT

## BEDSIDE TABLE

*A length of delicately embroidered cotton covers the bedside table, which together with candlelight and scented blossom creates a romantic affair. A swatch of ribbon makes a decorative feature of a light pull.*

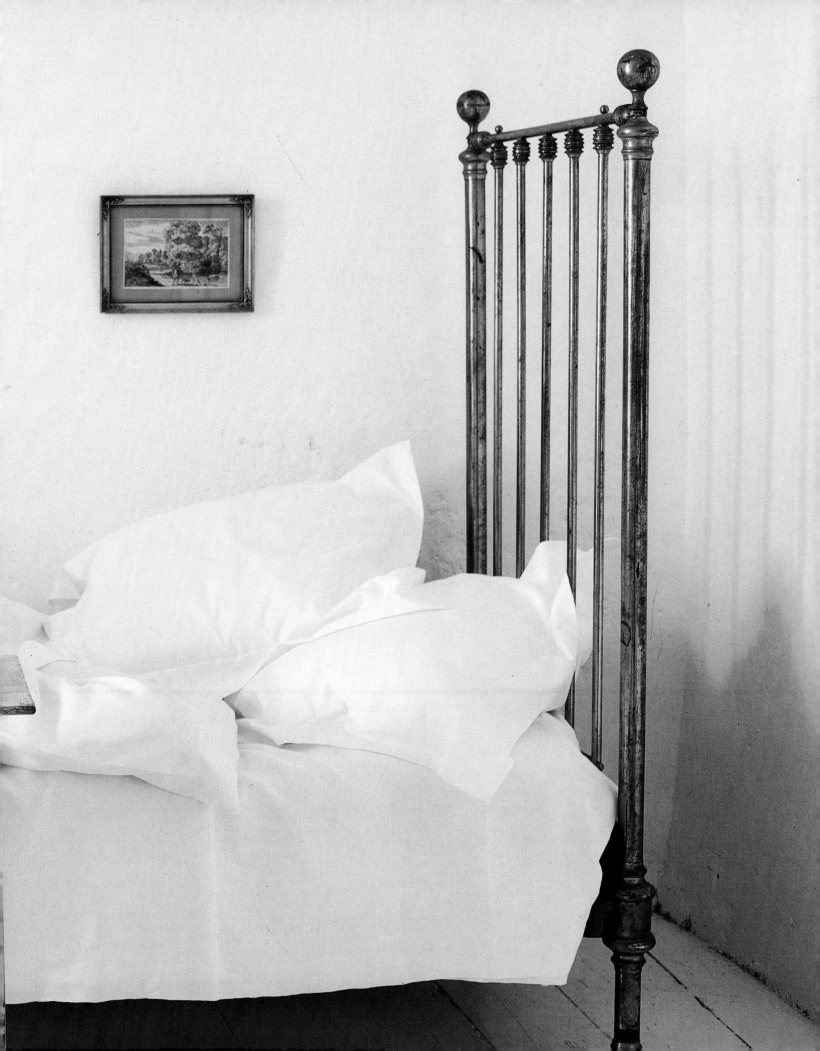

## BRIGHT WHITE

*In a north-facing bedroom, create as much light as possible. Floorboards are painted a glossy white and a large mirror propped against a wall reflects all the available light across the room. Crisp cotton piqué bedlinen contrasts well with the tarnished brass bedstead.*

The simplest of quilts can be made by placing a layer of wadding between two layers of cotton sheeting and binding the edges with narrow cotton strips. Mark the quilting lines on the top layer using tailor's chalk – diagonal lines are probably the most straightforward – then baste together the fabrics and machine stitch along the chalk marks. If you enjoy machine embroidery, develop patterns in the squares or leave plain, as you prefer. Alternatively, stitch intricate crewelwork patterns using white thick cotton thread or wool across the quilt. Of course, this type of stitching takes a great deal of time and patience to work, but the end result will be an heirloom to treasure over the years.

The most luxurious of pillows are large square ones with wonderfully wide borders around the edges, so-called Oxford-style pillowcases. They are very simple to make and with an envelope opening at the back require three pieces of fabric. Cut one to the size of your pillow with 25cm (10in) added to the dimensions (the front), and the other two pieces of fabric should both be the same width as the front, but half the length plus 15.5cm (6¼in) (the back). To prepare the back, machine stitch a hem 2.5cm (1in) along the side of each piece of fabric that will eventually be overlapping. Then baste the two back pieces together, overlapping the hemmed edges by 10cm (4in). Once basted together they should measure the same, both in length and width, as the piece of fabric which has been cut out for the front.

Pin and baste the front and back pieces together with right sides facing and then stitch taking a 15mm (½in) seam allowance. Turn right sides out through the envelop back, press and mark the stitching lines 11cm (4½in) in from the edge. Then sew together, forming the flange edging. If your sewing machine has satin stitch, use a narrow size as this is a pretty stitch on a pillowcase. For further decorative effect, appliqué lace panels to the front of the pillows – or trim with lengths of antique lace.

## CLEVER COMBINATIONS

*Framed pictures are simply and informally leant against the walls; an effortless way to display favourite prints, providing flexibility and, of course, avoiding the problem of nailing picture hooks in an unyielding wall.*

RIGHT

## MOVING FURNITURE

*If you are the proud owner of*

*a bed on wheels, move it*

*into the sun on a glorious*

*summer's day, flinging wide*

*the doors and windows. Crisp*

*embroidered linen, an old quilt*

*or two and a deep pile of*

*large, square pillows will*

*guarantee a blissful siesta.*

*Simple bleached cotton*

*curtains hang at the windows*

*to help filter strong rays of*

*sunlight. They are caught up*

*with ties of cotton tape.*

## THE LINEN STORE

*A capacious, built-in cupboard*

*is the perfect linen store –*

*plenty of room to pile neatly*

*pressed sets of bedlinen and*

*table linen, tied with pieces of*

*ribbon. The shelves are lined*

*with sheets of cotton edged*

*with lace – launder these*

*regularly to ensure your linens*

*remain perfectly clean.*

Another style of pillow that is really comfortable on a bed, especially if you enjoy a quiet bit of reading, is a bolster, so frequently used in France. A tied bolster cushion is particularly simple to make because it only involves working with one piece of fabric. For different finished effects, gather the fabric at the ends of the bolster by sewing on a button, tassel or rosette. Cut your piece of fabric so that it measures the length of the bolster pad plus the diameter of one end plus 6cm (2½in). The width of the fabric needs to measure the circumference of the bolster plus 6cm (2½in). For the ties that will ultimately be used to gather each end, cut two strips of fabric, each of which is 4cm (1⅝in) wide and the length of the main fabric.

To make, pin the long edges of the cover together with the right sides facing, and machine stitch taking a 15mm (½in) seam allowance. Press the seam open and turn right sides out. Also turn 15mm (½in) of fabric in at each end, pin and press. Make a double hem by turning in a further 2cm (¾in) of fabric at each end, then pin and machine stitch. Make up the fabric ties. Unpick the seam stitches where they overlap with the double hems at each end of the cover and feed one of the fabric ties around each end by attaching a safety pin to the end of each tie. Finally, insert the bolster pad, making sure it is central, and pull the fabric ties to gather the ends. Neaten by tying into bows.

## BEDROOM FURNISHINGS

Large, old-fashioned linen cupboards, dining buffets, and freestanding shelves cleverly disguised with knotted sheets (see pages 122-3) make unusual, and yet very decorative, pieces of furniture in a bedroom. Experiment by combining weathered pieces of painted furniture with more modern pieces, perhaps disguised with a particularly beautiful piece of fabric that you have been harbouring over the years, or painted to look deliberately old and faded.

RIGHT

## LIGHT AND SHADE

*This pretty arrangement sits*

*on a bedroom mantelpiece.*

*The delicately edged*

*watercoloured print of the*

*song thrush has been simply*

*mounted while awaiting a*

*frame. The decorative paper*

*lace is perfect used as*

*shelf edging.*

This paint technique is easily achieved by first painting the piece of furniture with a dark colour of thinned enamel varnish which is left to dry. Then dot blobs of vaseline over the top. Again, leave the vaseline to dry for at least 12 hours before painting on two different colours of emulsion – first, say, white, and then cream. The second coat of paint should be diluted with water so that the colour is not quite so dense. Then comes the fun part; after about 30 minutes, expose the layers of paint and enamel beneath using a cloth and scraper.

For the sweetest smelling bedlinen, run up small lavender bags using lace remnants or muslin or organza. Fill with dried lavender, or any other favourite mixture of pot pourri, and then gather the tops of the bags with narrow ribbons threaded through the hem. Placed in drawers and on shelves, the natural aromas will freshen newly washed linens and naturally repel insects.

## BEDROOM FURNISHINGS

*A few large, ruby red peony heads add a really dramatic touch to this white French chest of drawers. The simple moulding around each drawer front and on the mirror is truly typical of furniture from this part of the world, as are the little brass drawer handles. The worn paintwork only serves to enhance the charm of this piece.*

LEFT

## CHILD'S PLAY

*A bright and spacious*
*environment for a young child*
*– refreshingly white, the*
*accent of red makes a warm*
*contrast and the theme is*
*continued onto the appliquéd*
*blanket and small cotton*
*kimono hanging on the*
*cupboard door. The mosquito*
*net is both practical and fun,*
*while the worn Indian grass*
*matting is a perfect choice of*
*natural carpeting as it is*
*comfortable beneath little*
*bare feet.*

## CHILDREN'S ROOMS

A cosy appliquéd blanket, a calico patchwork quilt, a rag rug casually laid across the floor – making simple objects for a baby and child is extraordinarily rewarding. While your immediate reaction to creating a white room for the young might be one of surprise, when it comes to it, why not? All surfaces and items are washable, and a fresh white room is a peaceful place, conducive to contentment and calm, to be encouraged in all young children.

The classic American Colonial style has its roots particularly in Swedish and German folk art, and plain walls painted with a whitewash are a must for such a simple decorative style. Simple naive designs are stencilled in a repeating pattern above the skirting boards and around the doors and windows, or indeed on any other architectural feature that might be present. An attractive looped or rag rug finishes off the room with just the right sort of neutral background. So whether you want to set about creating a country style like this, or go for something even simpler – cool blue furnishings combined with white paintwork, for example, is a very popular look in France – here is the place to do it.

For soft furnishing details, an old worn white blanket, for example, can be quickly and easily revitalized by cutting it to child size. Letters and spots can then be cut from the remnants and blanket-stitched into place using brightly coloured wools. The end result is a charmingly naive, personalized blanket to wrap up in on a winter's night. Similarly, enliven a cotton kimono and pyjamas with even running stitches using a contrasting coloured embroidery thread.

To make a patchwork quilt for a cot, cut out enough small squares of calico or linen for the finished size, stitch them together and then neatly back with a single piece of fabric. For some simple decorative detailing, stitch long running stitches around each square using thick white cotton thread.

## SWEET DREAMS

*This small iron rocking cot*

*has been painted white and*

*filled with a tiny organza*

*frilled pillow and a small*

*calico patchwork quilt with*

*simple running stitches*

*adding form and texture. It is*

*worth remembering that*

*pillows should be used for*

*decoration only, babies need*

*to lie flat in their cots.*

# TENTED SHELVES

**WHAT YOU WILL NEED**

Freestanding shelves

2 single cotton sheets

Plastic carton or large

empty tin

Sand

2m (2yd) 2.5cm (1in)-wide

cotton tape

1 This tenting has to be the most incredibly simple way of dressing up freestanding shelves to give an attractive and sophisticated finish to what might otherwise be a stark bedroom feature. The sheets should be sufficiently long that you can tie a knot at the top and then drape them all the way down to the floor.

2 The rest of the work is then simply done by making the large knot at the top of the shelves. With the two sheets facing each other, right sides out, take each pair of corners, one in each hand, and tie in a half knot, and then tie again, also in a half knot. Neaten the ends by tucking them into the knot towards the back of the tent.

3 Drape the cover over the shelf and position a plastic carton or large empty tin filled with sand beneath the knot to give it some extra height, further enhancing the tent-like effect. Check that the bottom of the sheets drape gracefully on the floor and if you feel there is too much, turn up the excess into a hem. The two sheets should meet together at the back. If you prefer, they can be stitched together to avoid parting.

4 To finish off the tent, attach tiebacks a third of the way down at each front corner. Make the ties from the cotton tape cutting two 41cm (18in)-long strips for each tieback. Sew a strip to the front and one to the back on each side of the front corners and then simply tie neat bows when you want to keep the tent doors open.

# PICTURE FRAMES

**WHAT YOU WILL NEED**

Sepia photographs

Doilies

Spray adhesive

Clip frames

Scraps white card

Fountain pen

Brown ink

2.5cm (1in)-wide gummed

linen tape

1 The small sepia pictures featured here have been subtly mounted onto square doilies. White on white, the finished effect is pretty, the texture subtle. Before venturing any further with this project, choose your doily to fit the picture. Depending on what result you are intending to achieve, choose one which is only just larger than the photograph, or perhaps search out one that is much bigger, giving you a really generous border.

2 Using a spray adhesive and mask to cover your nose and mouth, fasten a white paper mount to the backing board and then stick the doily onto the paper ensuring you centre it and make sure it is straight. Then stick the picture in place, also centring and straightening it.

3 For a simple and attractive finishing touch, write a label on a separate piece of white card describing, say, who is in the picture or the year in which it was taken, and stick in place beneath the doily. For a good match with the sepia photograph, use brown ink. Then put the glass in place over the top and add the clips to hold it steady.

4 The finishing touch is the gummed linen strips that are fastened around the edge. Cut four strips, one for each side, wet the backs and then leave for about 15 seconds so that the strips become more malleable. Stick the strips on the frame so that 12mm ($\frac{1}{2}$in) appears at the front and the rest is folded to the back. Start on the left side and work around each side in a clockwise direction as shown in the illustration on the right.

# DAISY BRAIDED CURTAIN

**WHAT YOU WILL NEED**

5cm (2in)-wide

upholsterer's webbing

Ball of string

Large needle

Cream cotton thread

Curtain

Pins

Sewing machine

1 This charming daisy-chain braid adds decorative detail to the edge of a very simple natural linen curtain. The background for this edging is made from strips of the upholsterer's webbing which can be bought from any good haberdashers. Cut sufficient lengths of the webbing to fit the entire height of each curtain you are decorating.

2 To make the string design, start at one end of the webbing with your ball of string and needle and thread. First lay a length of string on the webbing to represent the daisy stem and couch this in place with the needle and cream cotton thread.

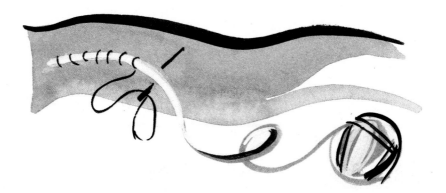

3 Then for each daisy head, fold the string around several times to make the petals and just catch it in place in the centre with several large over stitches. In this way, the petals stay soft and fall freely. If you prefer something a little more organized, you could of course couch each petal in place as with the stems. Repeat this simple stem-daisy-stem-daisy sequence along the webbing.

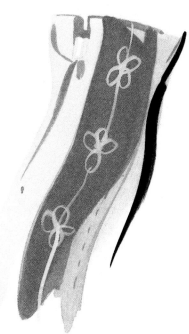

4 Pin and baste the webbing to the curtain(s), 12mm (½in) in from the edge, and then use a sewing machine to stitch it down firmly on both edges and around the ends. For a more formal setting, stitch the braid to a pelmet and tiebacks, or sew the string in designs made from straight lines such as zigzags or Greek keys.

# CHAPTER FIVE

# ROOMS FOR BATHING

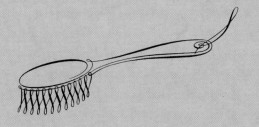

# ROOMS FOR BATHING

In a simple home, the bathroom is an uncluttered room where the focus of attention is the bath, the lavatory and the washbasin, with perhaps a bidet thrown in for good, clean measure. Don't distract the eye by bringing in other furniture or adding carpets and cushions, instead keep it functional and to the point. In France, this is just how bathrooms are decorated; commodious marble baths and basins, luxurious thick white towels hanging from a brass towel rail on the wall, and square chunks of olive oil soap, bristle brushes and natural sponges with which to ablute. However, a chair is always a useful item to have around in a bathroom, as is somewhere to store your linen, soaps and perhaps a pot plant or two.

Buy a generously proportioned washbasin that is shallow and broad with the taps set well back so that you can sluice water around without worrying about it flooding the floor. Recesses for soap and plugs are equally important for without them all those washing accoutrements become something of an irritation. Likewise, a large bath designed to soak in is a must. It needs to be long enough to accommodate a tall person and deep enough to hold plenty of soothing warm water to wash away the cares of the day.

Large baths are available in all the conventional materials, but for a more continental feel, look for a cast-iron bathtub with ball-and-claw feet or even a stone bath – although these are increasingly hard to find. In large, old-fashioned bathrooms, marble was a valued commodity as it is cool and hard-wearing. However, the expense of using such a material can be totally prohibitive. Instead, try your hand at a marble paint-effect on, say, the outside of a tin bath, or on wooden cupboard doors.

LEFT

## GENEROUS PROPORTIONS

*A really good sized mirror – carved and gilded like this one – makes a strong impact on an otherwise plain white bathroom. Notice the large woven natural linen towel which is fully absorbent. It is a really good alternative to the fluffy cotton ones we're used to, particularly after a summer's bath.*

## WALL AND FLOOR TILES

Another prerequisite of the simple bathroom are tiles on floor and walls; they help to retain the clean feel of such a room and are also suitably cool and restrained. To continue a continental, marbled theme, lay black and white marbled vinyl linoleum or tiles in a diamond chequered pattern with perhaps a narrow, mosaic-like border of smaller tiles around the edge. These sorts of tiles are very durable and they are easy to cut and lay, usually requiring an adhesive to keep them in place – consult the manufacturer's instructions.

On walls, white tiles make valuable splash-backs and surrounds for washbasins and bath alike. The amount of wall you choose to cover is, of course, entirely a personal choice but for baths that incorporate a shower you might well consider tiling all the way up the wall. If you are going to do the tiling yourself, remember that it is important that you plan the first row particularly carefully as untidy tiling can be irksome to the eye, especially when using plain tiles. The lines between need to be as regular as possible. So ensure that the first row is both level and square by first placing vertical and horizontal battens on the wall with masonry nails. When it comes to the actual tiling, always start in a corner and put in spacers to separate the tiles. Also, as you complete each row, check that it is horizontal.

You will invariably need to cut tiles for edges. Before cutting anything, mark the lines with a chinagraph pencil against a set-square, and if you need to do several to the same size do them all in one batch. Then cut straight lines with score-and-snap pliers or gently remove corners and curves with pincers and then smooth all edges with a tile file. Once the tiling is complete, wait at least 12 hours before removing the battens and spacers, and finally add grout in all the spaces, using a waterproof product, and also seal any gaps between the tiles and bath or basin with silicone caulk.

LEFT

PALE BLOSSOMS

*A fresh bloom or two*

*adds to the relaxed mood*

*of a bathroom.*

OPPOSITE

## SIMPLE STORAGE

*The simplest of storage units*

*can be made by building*

*supports from concrete*

*blocks painted white and*

*topped with a decorative*

*marble console top which can*

*occasionally be found in*

*antique shops or salvage*

*yards. A bath by candlelight*

*must be the best possible*

*way of relaxing after a*

*busy day.*

LEFT

## MARBLE CONTAINERS

*Great chunks of olive oil soap*

*and all essential bathroom*

*paraphernalia are tidily kept in*

*chunky marble dishes. Try*

*filling pretty stoppered jars*

*such as vinaigrette bottles*

*with favourite bath oils and*

*colognes.*

# SCALLOPED TABLECLOTH

**WHAT YOU WILL NEED**

**Plasticized cotton fabric**

**Dressmaker's scissors**

**Saucer**

**Ballpoint pen**

**Large coin**

**Embroiderer's scissors**

**Leather punch**

1 By cutting soft scallops around the edge of a plastic tablecloth you will instantly create something far more stylish. An added smaller scallop to the larger one makes it even more interesting – a charmingly simple version of traditional broderie anglaise. To start, cut your length of plasticized cotton fabric to size. Remember to add an allowance all the way around, because whether you are covering a round, square or rectangular table you will lose some of the fabric as you cut out the scallops.

2 To make the scallops, take a saucer and draw around half of it for each scallop. Draw on the back of the fabric with the ballpoint pen and work your way along each side if the cloth is square or rectangular, and for each corner draw around three quarters of the saucer.

## SCALLOPED TABLECLOTH

*The decorative scalloped*

*edges of this tablecloth are*

*reminiscent of traditional*

*broderie anglaise.*

3 Then, to make the smaller scallops within each scallop, take a large coin
and repeat as for step 2 on the previous page. For positioning the coin
at the top of each scallop, see the illustration below. When you have
completed marking-out, cut around the edge of the tablecloth using the
embroiderer's scissors.

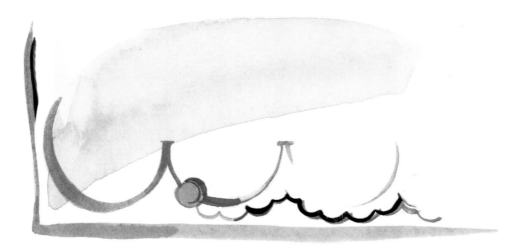

4 For the decorative holes, use a leather punch. On this tablecloth a series
of larger holes has been punched around the edge and then a row of
smaller ones. This is a very time-consuming task but don't worry too much
about precision – it is the general effect that is most noticeable. Of course,
you needn't feel restricted to punching holes around the border; you might
choose to develop flower designs to make a deeper border.

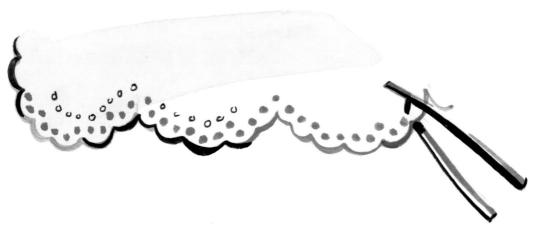

# CHAPTER SIX

# OUTDOOR LIVING

RIGHT

## PRACTICALITIES

*Tin and enamelware are the*

*perfect vessels for food*

*preparation, for dining off,*

*drinking from and washing-up*

*in on the beach. Solid and*

*hardwearing, they are also*

*light to carry.*

OPPOSITE

## RECYCLING
## BOTTLES

*Old glass bottles are very*

*stylish containers and can, of*

*course, be used again and*

*again and again. Fill them with*

*home-made cordials or*

*lemonade and seal with*

*a cork.*

between each, and then lay the other four over the top at 90 degrees to the first set. Again leave 15cm (6in) spaces between each strip. Pin the strips together and then sew firmly on a sewing machine using thick cotton thread. The end result is a neat ribbon effect and the holes let in changing shafts of light through the day.

To suspend the canopy, put a grommet into each corner of the canvas and tie the back to the trellis or to nails in the wall using nylon cord, and then prop up the front with collapsible tent poles with tapered points. For support, tie more nylon cord around the pole points and stake them firmly in the ground well away from the canopy.

If you have a large tree in your garden, a hanging canopy suspended from one of the main branches is a lovely alternative. The basis of a canopy like this is a frame of four 5cm (2in)-diameter wooden dowels, each 1.5m (5ft) long, hooked together into a square that hangs from the bough of the tree. To make the canopy, first cut four 1.5 x 3m (5 x 10ft) canvas panels, each of which should be hemmed along one of the short edges to create a channel for each of the dowels. Feed the dowels through and then lay out them in a square, with the canvas panels extending away.

To join the frame, attach a screw eye to both ends of each dowel. Then cut two 2.4m (8ft) lengths of nylon clothesline and tie a metal snap hook to each end. Each of the four snap hooks then clips into the screw eyes at the ends of two dowels, connecting one dowel to the next to link them into a square. Each nylon line runs diagonally across the square, but before being hooked to its opposite corner, pass each line through a heavy metal ring which will ultimately be used to suspend the canopy.

The moment of canopy hanging has now arrived. Snap-hook the central ring to a 9m (30ft) length of 3-strand, 10mm (³⁄₈in) nautical line and run this up

LEFT

## OUTDOOR BATHING

*In the privacy of your sun-deck take a refreshing outdoor bath on a hot summer's day. Here a zinc bathtub is ready and waiting, as are the white cotton waffle towels. A Lloyd Loom chair is fashionably covered with a flirty loose cover made in an eminently cosy and practical white towelling.*

through a standard pulley hung on a strong, short chain from the bough. Run the other end of the line down from the pulley to a metal cleat fixed to the tree trunk at waist height, where the line is secured. You are now able to raise and lower the canopy with ease by pulling the line through the pulley. The nylon lines of the frame should form a taut, level pyramid when the canopy is suspended and the ceiling can easily be altered to suit the height you want. Keep the bottom end of each panel in place by making a hem of 5cm (2in) and adding a grommet at each corner. Tie 60cm (2ft) lengths of the nylon cord to each corner and stake them out so that the panels are taut in wide, tent-like wings.

## OUTDOOR FURNISHINGS

The best furniture to use outside is items that are simple and sturdy, made either of wood or metal. A metal-topped café table, for example, is to the point, or for something really durable use a marble top sitting on solid cast-iron legs. Seats, too, should be both comfortable and durable. Small upright wooden kitchen chairs, wood and metal chairs with slats, benches, and battered wicker or cane chairs made comfortable with squab cushions are all perfect for a spot of al fresco dining. For some post-prandial lounging, wheel out the day bed, relax on a colonial chair-bed or suspend a hammock between two shady trees.

## DOWN AT THE BEACH

Outdoor living need not be limited to the garden, and a day or more at the seaside can be just as invigorating. If you like your home comforts and a beach hut is not to hand, go for something a little more unusual and take a tent with you. White canvas is, as ever, cool and comfortable, and with a director's chair or two, some cushions and a simple cotton dhurry to keep the sand at bay, what more could you ask for?

LEFT

## IN THE HEAT
## OF THE DAY

*An outsize cotton umbrella*

*will keep the sizzling sun from*

*burning, or a bracing wind*

*from chilling you as you*

*quietly sit, watching the*

*waves inexorably move their*

*way up or down the beach*

*before you take a swim.*

# TEMPLATES

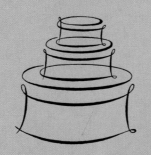

# TEMPLATES

The templates that appear on the following pages are for some of the projects in this book.

They are: overleaf: Floral Floorcloth *(see pages 74-7)*

pages 182-3: Bonbon Boxes *(see pages 46-9)*

pages 184-5: Leafy Lampshade *(see pages 42-5)*

## ENLARGING TEMPLATES

As you will have your own ideas about how large or small you wish each project to be, you may need to enlarge the templates. If you have access to a photocopier with an enlarging facility, this is the easiest way to enlarge a template. But if you don't, then use the conventional square method. To do this, draw a grid of squares over the relevant template and then on a separate piece of paper draw a duplicate grid of squares but this time larger so that the same number of squares covers the larger area. Then it is simply a matter of meticulously copying the design square by square.

## TRANSFERRING DESIGNS

To transfer a design to the relevant surface, trace it onto tracing paper with a soft pencil and then go over the lines on the back of the paper with the same pencil. Position the tracing paper on the surface and once more draw over the top of the paper and the pencil marks on the bottom will be transferred. Alternatively, for simpler outlines, trace the shape, cut it out and then draw around it once it has been positioned on the surface you will be working on.

# FLORAL FLOORCLOTH

*(see pages 74-5)*

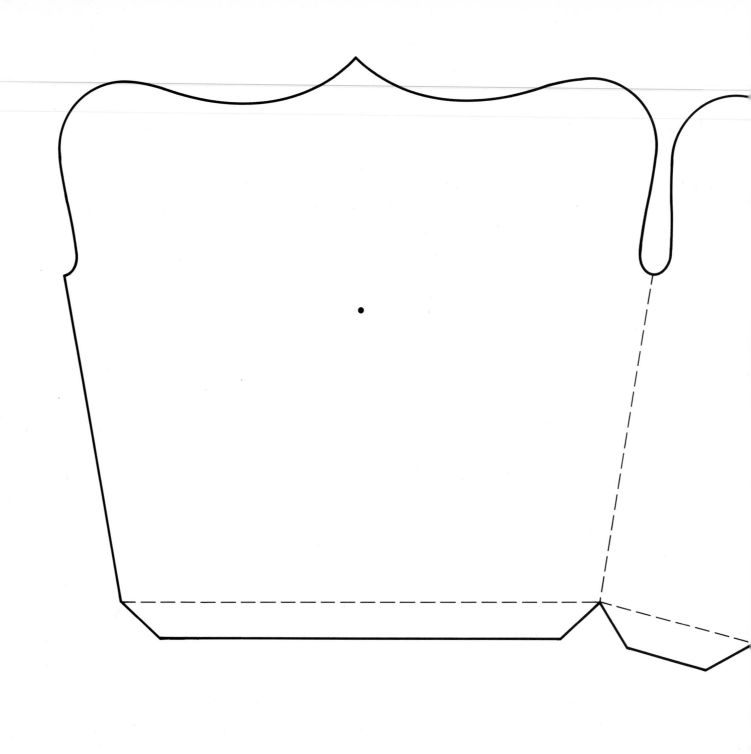

BONBON BOX BASE

*(cut two, one slightly smaller than the other)*

BONBON BOXES

*(see pages 48-9)*

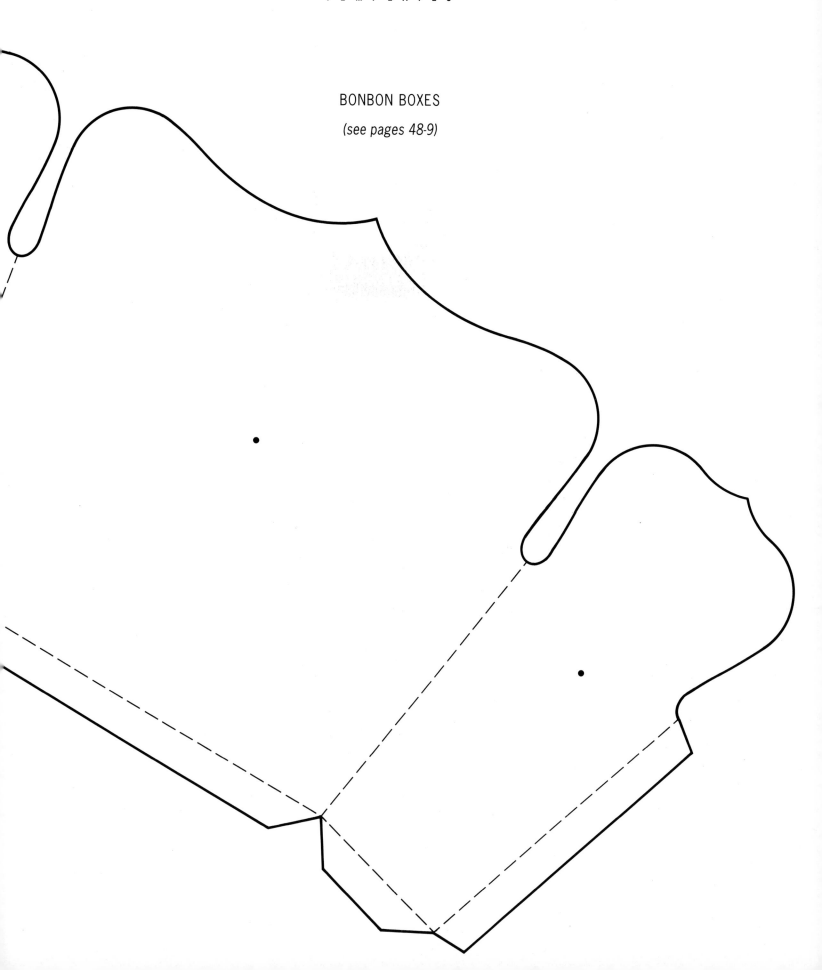

# LEAFY LAMPSHADE

*(see pages 42-5)*

# SUPPLIERS

This is by no means a fully comprehensive list of suppliers, but my own personal list of favourite haunts where I find the things that I love, and many of which feature throughout this book.

## Antiques

ANTIQUES AND THINGS
91 Eccles Road, London SW11
0171 350 0597
*French decorative items. Specializes in curtain and lighting accessories.*

HILARY BATSTONE
51 Kinnerton Street, London SW1
0171 259 6070
*Decorative furniture, textiles and accessories. Large stock of antique curtains.*

BAZAR
82 Golbourne Road, London W10
0181 969 6262
*Nineteenth-century French and continental furnishings, including garden furniture with a rustic flavour.*

DECORATIVE LIVING
55 New King's Road, London SW6
0171 736 5623
*Rustic French and unique reproduced furniture, and lots of bric-a-brac.*

NICOLE FABRE
592 King's Road, London SW6
0171 384 3112
*Specializes in French textiles and furniture and English country furniture.*

JUDY GREENWOOD
657 Fulham Road, London SW6
0171 736 6037
*Specializes in French painted furniture. Also antique quilts and textiles.*

MARK MAYNARD
651 Fulham Road, London SW6
0171 731 3533
*Varied range, including wood and painted furniture.*

MYRIAD ANTIQUES
131 Portland Road, London W11
0171 229 1709
*French country and battered antiques and also many other decorative pieces including faux bamboo.*

PAVILION ANTIQUES
(by appointment only)
01225 722522
*French antiques and textiles especially linens, enamelware and pottery.*

PIMPERNEL & PARTNERS
596 Kings Road, London SW6
0171 731 2448
*Decorative French antiques.*

BRYONY THOMASSON
(by appointment only)
0171 731 3693
*Antiques, decorative and hand-woven textiles, rustic clothing and objects. Also at 283 Westbourne Grove, Portobello Rd, London W11 (Saturday only).*

TOBIAS AND THE ANGEL
68 White Hart Lane, London SW13
0181 878 8902
*English country antiques.*

## Art shops

GREEN & STONE
259 King's Road, London SW3
0171 352 0837
*Long-established artists' suppliers.*

PAPERCHASE
213 Tottenham Court Road,
London WC2
0171 580 8496
*Wide range of papers, stationary, ribbons, etc
Items sent by mail order.*

## Bathrooms

ASTON MATTHEWS
141-147A Essex Rd,
London N1
0171 226 3657
*A fully comprehensive range of cast-iron baths, taps, showers, wash basins and WCs.*

THE WATER MONOPOLY
16-18 Lonsdale Road,
London NW6
0171 624 2636
*Restoration of French antiquated bathroom fittings and accessories.*

## Bedlinen

THE WHITE COMPANY
0171 385 7988
*Cotton and linen duvets, pillows, bedspreads, tablecloths, towels, bathrobes and gifts – all in white. Items sent by mail order.*

## Decorating shops

THE BLUE DOOR
77 Church Rd, London SW13
0181 748 9785
*Eighteenth-century reproduction and
original Swedish furniture, textiles
and accessories.*

THE CONRAN SHOP
Michelin House, 81 Fulham Road,
London
0171 589 7401
*The latest in contemporary design.*

DESIGNERS GUILD
267-271 & 277 King's Rd,
London SW3
0171 351 5775
*Richly coloured fabrics, furniture and
other decorative items.*

HABITAT
Branches throughout the UK
0645 334433

IKEA
Branches throughout the UK
0181 451 5566

CATH KIDSTON
8 Clarendon Cross, London W11
0171 221 4000
*Household effects and interior
design, with an emphasis on the
1950s.*

JOHN LEWIS
278-306 Oxford street, London W1
0171 629 7711
*And branches throughout the UK*

## Ethnic shops

JOSS GRAHAM ORIENTAL
TEXTILES
10 Eccleston Street,
London SW1
0171 730 4370
*A comprehensive selection of
decorative textiles, ceramics,
jewellery and clothing from India.*

DAVID WAINWRIGHT
251 Portobello Road, London W11
0171 792 1988
*Indian furniture and accessories.
Also at 28 Rosslyn Hill, Hampstead,
London NW3 0171 431 5900.*

## Fabrics

CELIA BIRTWELL
71 Westbourne Park Road,
London W2 0171 221 0877
*Printed textiles, ranging from sheer
silks to cotton and velvet.*

CHELSEA TEXTILES DESIGN
7 Walton Street, London SW1
0171 584 0111
*Hand-embroidered fabrics based on
antique designs as well as
contemporary ranges.*

DESIGNERS GUILD
277 King's Road, London SW3
0171 351 5775
*Modern, coloured fabric, furniture
and other decorative items.*

FIRIFISS FABRICS GALLERY
278-280 Brompton Road,
London SW3
0171 589 4778

NATURAL FABRIC COMPANY
Wessex Place, 127 High Street,
Hungerford, Berkshire
01488 684002
*Indian cottons, Irish linen and English
cloth.*

MACCULLOCH & WALLIS
25 Dering Street, London W1
0171 629 0311
*Haberdashery and fabrics of all
kinds, especially cottons and linen.*

MALABAR COTTON COMPANY
The Coach House, Bakery Place,
119 Altenburg Gardens,
London SW11
0171 978 5848
*Indian hand-woven cotton.*

IAN MANKIN
271 Wandsworth Bridge Road,
London SW6
0171 371 8825

*Specializes in simple fabric designs,
especially checked, and also striped
tickings.*

OSBORNE & LITTLE
304-308 King's Road, London SW3
0171 352 1456
*Colourful modern printed and woven
fabrics.*

RUSSELL & CHAPPLE
23 Monmouth Street, London WC2
0171 836 7521
*Suppliers of artists' canvas and
linens.*

GEORGE WEIL
18 Hanson Street, London W1
0171 580 3763
*Wide range of basic undyed fabrics
and dyes and paints.*

WHALEYS
Harris Court, Great Horton,
Bradford, West Yorkshire
01274 576718
*Calicos, cotton, canvases and silks
in white, natural and black.*

## Flooring

CRUCIAL TRADING
77 Westbourne Park Rd, London W2
0171 221 9000
*Specializes in natural fibre flooring
and coir matting.*

FIRED EARTH
Twyford Mill, Oxford Rd, Adderbury,
Oxfordshire
01295 812088
*Huge selection of ceramic tiles. Also*
*at 21 Battersea Square, London*
*SW11 0171 924 2272 and*
*102 Portland Road, London W11*
*0171 221 4825.*

SINCLAIR TILL FLOORING
791-793 Wandsworth Road,
London SW8
0171 720 0031
*Traditional linoleum and hardwood*
*floors as well as carpets and natural*
*floor coverings.*

**Framing**
FIX-A-FRAME
280 Old Brompton Road,
London SW5
0171 370 4189

**Ceramics and decorative objects**
JESSICA BOURDON SMITH
4 Hobhouse Court, Suffolk Street,
London, SW1Y
0171 930 3523
*Specializes in decorative objects.*

JACQUI ROCHE
Studio 4, Great Western Studios,
Great Western Road, London W9
0171 266 1776

*Pottery workshop producing a range*
*of beakers, jugs and vases.*

ANN SILVESTRIN
0171 403 5170
*White shapely ceramic bowls and*
*vases.*

ANNA TORTORELLI
Unit 315, Clerkenwell workshops,
31 Clerkenwell Close,
London EC1
0171 490 8373
*Jewellery and metal designs.*

**Garden Furniture**
CLIFTON LITTLE VENICE
3 Warwick Place, London W9
0171 289 7894
*Range of garden furniture and*
*accessories.*

**Kitchens and Tableware**
DIVERTIMENTI
139-141 Fulham Road,
London SW6
0171 581 8065
*Stocks a wide range of stylish*
*kitchen equipment.*

HAYLOFT WOODWORK
3 Bond Street, London W4
0181 747 3510
*Custom-built kitchens, bathrooms,*
*wardrobes and other furniture.*

LEON JAEGGI
77 Shaftesbury Avenue, London W1
0171 434 4545
*Retail and manufacture of all basic*
*catering kitchen equipment.*

DAVID MELLOR
4 Sloane Square, London SW1
0171 730 4259
*Kitchen equipment and cutlery.*

NEWCASTLE FURNITURE
COMPANY
128 Walham Green Court,
Moore Park Road, London SW6
0171 386 9203
*Manufacturers of traditional-style*
*kitchens in solid wood.*

OLD TOWN
32 Elm Hill, Norwich, Norfolk
01603 628 100
*Old enamelled kitchen equipment,*
*checked fabrics and linen.*

SUMMERILL & BISHOP
100 Portland Road, London W11
0171 221 4566
*Everything for your kitchen.*

**Lighting**
LONDON LIGHTING COMPANY
135 Fulham Road, London SW3
0171 589 3612
*Modern lighting.*

**Paint**
BIOFA NATURAL PAINTS
5 School Road, Kidlington,
Oxfordshire *(mail order)*
01865 374 964
*A full range of environmentally*
*friendly household paint.*

FARROW & BALL
33 Uddens Trading Estate,
Wimbourne,
Dorset BH21 7NL
01202 876 141
*National Trust range of paints.*

JOHN OLIVER
33 Pembridge Road,
London W11
0171 727 3735
*A wide range of specialist paints and*
*wallpapers (mail order available).*

**Photographic Prints**
THE SPECIAL PHOTOGRAPHERS
GALLERY
21 Kensington Park Road,
London W11
0171 221 3489

**Tents**
RELUM LTD
Carlton Park Industrial Estate,
Kelsale, Saxmundham,
Suffolk IP17 2NL
01728 603271

# INDEX

# ACKNOWLEDGMENTS

The author would like to thank the following suppliers for their help with the photographs in this book:

pp7-8 The Blue Door (cupboard, jardinere); p16 Myriad Antiques (chair); p19 Chelsea Textiles (cushions); pp20-1 Judy Greenwood (cupboard), Hilary Batstone (metal chair), Tobias and the Angel (upholstered chair), The Blue Door (accessories), Clifton Little Venice (table); pp24-5 Celia Birtwell (blind fabric), cushions made by Caroline Bickett-Harris, Crucial Trading (mat); p26 The Conran Shop (chair, accessories), Pierre Frey (fabric); p27 Paperchase (paper); p34 The Blue Door (glass pots); p39 The London Lighting Co (lamp); p41 blind made by Caroline Bickett-Harris, Firifiss (fabric); p42 Myriad Antiques (table); p54 Cath Kidston (chairs), Pavilion Antiques (china, linen); p58 Divertimenti (tea cup and saucer); p60 Pavilion Antiques (linen); p64 The Blue Door (embroidered muslin); p67 Pavilion Antiques (china); p70 bean balls made by Simone Bendix, The Blue Door (plate); p78 Jacqui Roach (ceramics); p80 Cath Kidston (chair), Pavilion Antiques (breadboard); p85 Summerill and Bishop (baskets); p86 Old Town (enamel tins, accessories); p87 Cath Kidston (chair); pp88-9 Jacqui Roach (ceramics); p91 The Blue Door (cutlery); p93 Habitat (chairs, wooden boxes, accessories), Newcastle Furniture Co (kitchen table), Designers Guild (glasses); pp94-5 Special Photographers Gallery (photograph), Jacqui Roach (ceramics); p97 Wells Reclamation (cupboard); p104 Designers Guild (linen); p106 Chelsea Textiles (tablecloth); p107 The Blue Door (quilt, mat); p108 Myriad Antiques (table), Hilary Batstone (quilt), The White Co (bedlinen); p110 Myriad Antiques (buffet), Hilary Batstone (chairs); p117 Decorative Living (chest of drawers); pp118-19 The Blue Door (blanket, floral fabric, lamp), Ikea (bear, mosquito net), Millenium (chair), Designers Guild (blind fabric), Myriad Antiques (upholstered child's chair); p121 Anna Tortorelli (copper sheep); p128 Pavilion Antiques (linen curtains), Designers Guild (rag dolls), Crucial Trading (rush matting); pp136-7 The Water Monopoly (bath, accessories), Sinclair Till (floor); p140 Jessica Bourdon-Smith (papier mache bowl); p142 David Wainwright (marble dishes), The Blue Door (pewter sconce); pp154-5 The Blue Door (tablecloth); pp158-9 Relum (tent), Pavilion Antiques (stool, linens); p160 Pavilion Antiques (metal table); p164 The Blue Door (bolster cover); p169 Pavilion Antiques (umbrella).